BEFORE THE
DINOSAURS

ISBN 0-590-45874-4

Text copyright © 1996 by Miriam Schlein.
Illustrations copyright © 1996 by Michael Rothman
All rights reserved. Published by Scholastic Inc.

12 11 10 9 8 7 6 5 4 3 2 1   6 7 8 9/9 0 1/0

Printed in the U.S.A.   09

First Scholastic printing, November 1996

The display type was set in Bostonia
The text type was set in Plantin
The illustrations are acrylic paintings
Design by Debora Smith

BEFORE THE DINOSAURS

by Miriam Schlein

illustrated by Michael Rothman

SCHOLASTIC INC.

New York Toronto London Auckland Sydney

Millions of years ago, the world was full of dinosaurs.

Some ate meat. Some ate plants.
Some were big. Some were small.
Where did the dinosaurs come from?
How did they begin to be?
What was there, *before* the dinosaurs?

Long before the dinosaurs,
hundreds of millions of years before,
seas covered most of the earth.
In the seas there were sponges, and corals, and snails,
and flat, hard-shelled creatures called **trilobites** (TRY-lo-bites).

6

After a while, there were fish.

They were not like the fish we know.

They had a little hole for a mouth.

They couldn't open or close it. They just sucked in their food.

These first fish are called **agnathans** (ag-NATH-ans).

That's how it was more than 500 million years ago.

Any dinosaurs yet?

No.

Nothing even like them.

Millions of years went by.
There were lots of fish now. Different kinds of fish.
Some were more like the fish we know;
fish with teeth and mouths that could open and close.
There were big sea scorpions that ate the fish.
There were even sharks.

Then, for the first time ever, plants began to grow
on the land. This was 400 million years ago.
Is *this* when the dinosaurs showed up?
No. Not yet.
This was the Age of Fishes.
Not the Age of Dinosaurs.

But something else showed up.
It was a special kind of fish.
Fish with super-strong muscles in their fins.
What did they do with these super-strong fins?
They did something no other fish ever did.
They crawled up onto the land!
These special fish are called **lobe-fins**.

As you know, and I know,
most fish die if they leave the water
because they can't breathe air.
The lobe-fins developed lungs so they *could* breathe air.
One lobe-fin is called **Eusthenopteron** (yoos-then-OP-ter-on).

Today, there are still relatives of the
lobe-fins. We call them **lungfish**. They
live in South America, Africa, and
Australia.

Why did the lobe-fins come up out of the water?
Maybe it was to snap up insects along the shore.
It was also getting to be more dangerous in the water.
Remember, there were sharks.
There was also **Dunkleosteus** (dunk-el-OST-e-us)—
a giant fish, 30 feet long, with sharp tooth-like jaws.

More and more,
lobe-fins muscled their way up onto the land.
And at some point, from these unusual fish,
a new kind of animal developed—
the kind we call **amphibians** (am-FIB-ee-ins).
This happened about 350 million years ago.

Amphibians are animals that live
part of their life in water
and part of their life on land.
Ichthyostega (ik-thee-oh-STEEG-a) was one of the first amphibians.
Do you see how it is different from a lobe-fin?
It has real legs. And feet.
Much better than fins for walking.

In some ways, amphibians were still like fish.
They laid their eggs in water.
Their babies (tadpoles) grew up in the water
and were like little fish at first.
They grew legs only later on.
So amphibians had to live close to water.

We still have amphibians
today. Frogs. Toads.
Salamanders.

Now the Age of Fishes was coming to an end.
Though, of course, there were still fish—lots of them.
And soon—if you want to call millions of years "soon"—
there were all kinds of different amphibians.

Eryops (ER-ee-ops) had a thick,
torpedo-shaped body. It lived
in the swamps and ate fish.

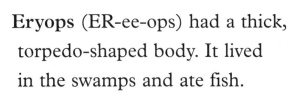

Eogyrinus (ee-o-gy-RINE-us)
was 15 feet long. It looked like
a gigantic eel with feet.

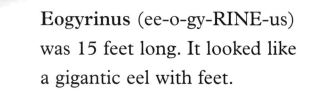

Diplocaulus (dip-luh-CALL-is)
was 3 feet long. It had a strange,
triangular-shaped head.

Seymouria (see-MOOR-ee-uh) was only
2 feet long. But it had pretty strong legs,
and spent most of its time on land.
(It has this name because it was
discovered in Seymour, Texas.)

Now tropical forests covered the land.
Giant ferns grew 100 feet tall.
Any dinosaurs there? No. Not yet.
But the forests weren't empty.
A new kind of animal appeared.
The kind of animal we call **reptiles** (REP-tiles).

Hylonomus (hy-lo-NOM-us) was one of the first reptiles.
It lived about 300 million years ago.
Hylonomus means "wood-dweller."
It was given this name because skeletons
were found inside hollow tree stumps.

How is a reptile different from an amphibian?
Is it bigger? Stronger? Not always.
The main difference is in the kind of eggs it lays.
Amphibian eggs are soft. They would dry out on land.
They have to be laid in water or in a damp place.
They get their nourishment from the water.

Reptile eggs are not like that.
A reptile egg has a shell to protect it.
The moisture and nourishment for
the baby are all *inside* the shell.
So reptiles can lay their eggs on land.

Was that important?
Yes. It meant that reptiles did not have to live close
to water, like amphibians.
They could move into the forest,
where there were fewer enemies
and there was less competition for food.

Many different kinds of reptiles developed.
They lived in different places.

Edaphosaurus (e-DAFF-oh-saur-us)
was a reptile with a "sail" on its back.
What good is a sail on a reptile?
Heat from the sun was stored in the sail,
and released later on, when needed.
(It was prehistoric solar heating!)

Dimetrodon (dye-MET-roh-don)
was a sharp-toothed meat-eating reptile
that sometimes attacked Edaphosaurus.

22

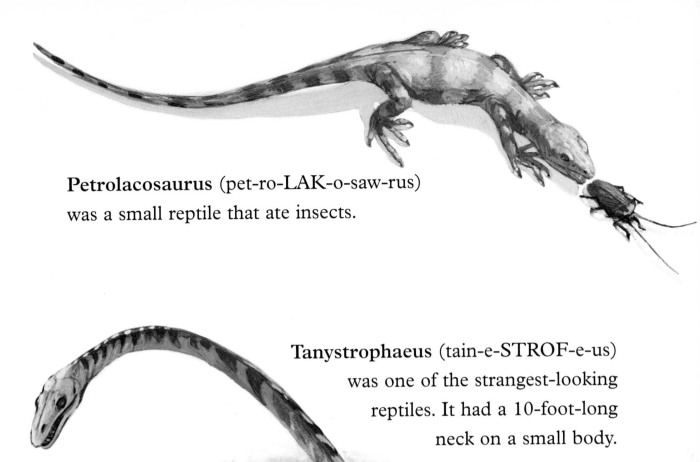

Petrolacosaurus (pet-ro-LAK-o-saw-rus) was a small reptile that ate insects.

Tanystrophaeus (tain-e-STROF-e-us) was one of the strangest-looking reptiles. It had a 10-foot-long neck on a small body.

How can new animals keep on appearing? Where did these reptiles come from?

They developed from the amphibians,
who developed from the lobe-fins,
who developed from the fish
who swam long ago in the seas.

How can this happen?
How can one kind of animal develop into another?

All this time, the earth had been changing.
It was not as warm as it once was. It was drier.
There was less water, more land.
In many places, there were now thick forests
where once there had been watery swamps.

As the earth keeps changing,
over long periods of time, many animals change, too.
They change in ways that help them survive
in a different kind of world.
They develop in ways
that will help them get food
and protect themselves.

We call this kind of changing *evolution*.

After a while, a special type of reptile appeared.
We call those reptiles **therapsids** (ther-AP-sids).

Some therapsids were small and timid.
Galepus (GAIL-e-pus) was only
about 10 inches long and
ate insects.

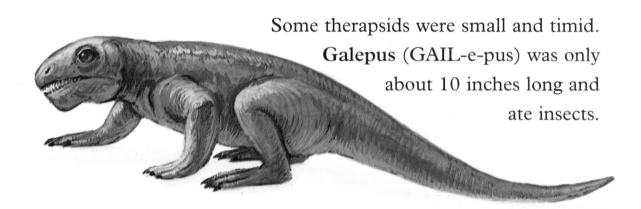

Others were more fierce. **Lycaenops** (ly-SEEN-ops)
was a meat-eater with teeth like daggers.
(Its name means "wolf-face.")

Lystrosaurus (liss-tro-SAUR-us) wandered in big herds. They dug for plants and cracked seeds with their beaks.

What was special about the therapsids?

Reptiles usually wriggle, or waddle.

Their legs sprawl out to the side.

(The word "reptile" means "to creep, to crawl.")

Therapsids were not like that.

In some ways they were more like mammals than reptiles.

Their bodies were higher off the ground.

Their legs were tucked more under the body,

more like a horse or a dog than an alligator.

Some even had hair, or at least a few whiskers.

(Reptiles usually have scales, not hair.)

The name therapsid means "mammal-like."

One kind of therapsid that had hair was the
massetognathus (mass-a-tog-NATH-us).
It was about the size of a cat.

A mammal is a warm-blooded vertebrate
(an animal with a backbone) that has hair,
and nourishes its young with milk.

In time, the therapsids led to the mammals we know today:
the dogs, cats, bears, bats, and the humans—to you and to me.
But *not* to the dinosaurs.

So many millions of years have passed.
We *must* be getting close to dinosaur-time.
You're right. We are. But not just yet.

29

About 240 million years ago,
another type of reptile appeared.
Thecodonts (THEEK-uh-donts)
had a different kind of teeth.
Their name means "socket-tooth."

Some thecodonts were big crocodile-like creatures.
Others were smaller and lived on land.
They are called **pseudosuchians** (soo-doh-SOOK-ee-uns),
which means "false crocodile."

Euparkeria (yoo-par-KER-ia) was a pseudosuchian.
It was small—only about 3 feet long.
It depended on good legwork to survive—
to catch its own food
or to dash off from an enemy.
Sometimes, it even got up on its back legs to sprint faster.

It's this little sprinter—or some other pseudosuchian like it—
that developed into a new special kind of reptile:
the kind we call **dinosaurs**.

Eoraptor (EE-o-rap-tor) was one of the first dinosaurs.
It was discovered in South America.
It was a small meat-eater about 3 feet long.
It lived about 228 million years ago.

How were dinosaurs different from other reptiles?
It's not that they were bigger. Some were not.
Or fiercer. Many were not.
An important difference had to do with their legs.

Dinosaur legs were *directly* under the body,
not sprawled off to the side.
Those right-under-the-body legs
supported the body better.
They made it possible, later on, for some dinosaurs
to become so gigantic.
(They would not have been able to hold up all that weight
with legs that sprawled off to the side!)
Their knee and ankle and hip bones were a bit different, too.
The way the bones joined together made it possible
for dinosaurs to take longer steps
and become better walkers and runners
than other reptiles.

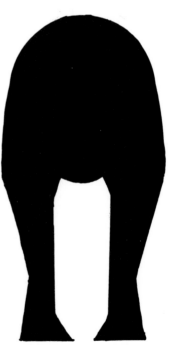

Some thecodont legs sprawled
out to the side.

Dinosaur legs were directly
under the body.

With legs that were right under its body, a dinosaur could walk and run better than other reptiles.

35

Soon—if you want to call millions of years "soon"—
there were all kinds of dinosaurs roaming the world.

Dinosaurs as tall as five-story buildings . . .
Dinosaurs that laid eggs as big as footballs . . .
Dinosaurs with beaks like ducks or horns like rhinos.
Some big. Some small.
Some fierce hunters.
Some that munched on plants.

The Age of Dinosaurs lasted for about 150 million years.

And it could not have happened
without the other reptiles . . .

and the amphibians before
the reptiles . . .

and the lobe-fins before
the amphibians . . .

and the fish with holes
for mouths . . .

and all the little creatures that
drifted in the ancient seas
before the dinosaurs.

TIME CHART

PALEOZOIC ERA

WHEN?	WHO lived then?	WHAT was earth like?
Cambrian, Ordovician, Silurian Periods [590 to 408 mya*]	Jawless fish (agnathans) Sponges, coral, trilobites Small sea scorpions	Most of earth covered with water.
Devonian Period [408 to 360 mya]	Fish with jaws First sharks Lobe-fins come up on land. First amphibians appear.	First plants grow on land.
Carboniferous Period [360 to 286 mya]	First reptiles	Forests. Land is low. No mountains. Today's coal deposits form.
Permian Period [286 to 248 mya]	Many different reptiles develop. Therapsids appear (mammal-like reptiles). Thecodonts appear.	Land not so flat. There are wet and dry seasons now. Land is still one big land mass called Pangaea. There are not yet separate continents. Glaciers in southern hemisphere.

* mya means millions of years ago

MESOZOIC ERA

WHEN?	WHO lived then?	WHAT was earth like?
Triassic Period [248 to 213 mya]	At the beginning, still many early reptiles and therapsids. First dinosaurs appear. First mammals appear. First pterodactyls appear.	Big land mass Pangaea is just starting to split apart. No grass yet. No flowers. More parts of earth drier than before.

By the end of Triassic Period, early types of reptiles are extinct. THE AGE OF DINOSAURS HAS ARRIVED.